Timeline

of

Pune

ROHAN VISHWAS JADHAV

Copyright © 2025 Rohan Vishwas Jadhav

Made with ❤ on the Notion Press Platform

www.notionpress.com

To The Family

Contents

Acknowledgement and References

It is a privilege to get an opportunity to express gratitude towards one's own teachers and authors that wrote extensively about Pune, feeling immensely grateful for this compilation of Timeline of Pune, covering **some or few** important milestones in the History of Pune.

Reports

1. Burrows G. R. S., Brigadier-General, Quartermaster-General, Routes in the Bombay Presidency, 1876

2. Clunes John, Itinerary and Directory for Western India, Calcutta, 1826.

3. Pune Nagar Sanshodhan Grantha, Vol. 1,2,3,4, Bharat Sanshodhan Mandal, Pune, 1942, 1943,1946,1952.

4. Report on proceedings at the Conference held at Poona 1865, Public Works Department, Government of Bombay, 1866

5. Sardesai G. S., Poona Residency Correspondence, Vol. 7, Poona Affairs, 1801-1810, Bombay, 1940.

Administrative Reports

1. The Administration Reports of the Poona Municipality for the Years 1879-80, 1885-86, 1886-87, 1888-89, 1889-90, 1891-92, 1893-94, 1894-95, 1895-96, 1896-97, 1897-98, 1899-1900, 1901-1902, 1906-07, 1907-08, 1908-09, 1913-14, 1916-17, 1917-18, 1918-19, 1919-1920, 1920-21, 1922-23, 1923-24, 1924-25, 1925-26, 1926-27, 1927-28, 1928-29, 1931-32, 1933-34, 1939-40.

Surveys

1. A Survey of Motor-Bus Transportation in Six Districts of the Bombay Presidency, GIPE, Poona, 1935.

2. Gadgil D. R., A survey of The Marketing of Fruit in Poona, 1933.

3. Gadgil D.R., Poona: A Socio-Economic Survey, Part I Economic, Gokhale Institute of Politics and Economics, Pune, 1945.

4. Gadgil D.R., Poona: A Socio-Economic Survey, Part II Social, Gokhale Institute of Politics and Economics, Pune, 1952.

5. Gadgil D.R., Poona: A Socio-Economic Survey, Part III Employment pattern, Gokhale Institute of Politics and Economics, Pune, 1956.

6.   Joshi Madhukar, Problem of Live-Stock in Poona District with Special reference to Marketing- A Survey, GIPE, Poona, 1948.

Gazetteers

1.   Gazetteer of the Bombay Presidency, Vol. XVIII, Part-I, II, III, 1885.

2.   Gazetteer of Bombay Presidency, Vol. XVIII-B: Poona and Bhor, 1921.

3.   Imperial Gazetteer of India, Provincial Series, Bombay Presidency, Vol. I, II, 1909.

4.   Gazetteer of Bombay State, District Series Vol. XX, 1954.

5.   Gazetteers of the Maharashtra State, Pune District (Supplementary), Government of Maharashtra, Mumbai, 1984.

Books

1.   Choksey R. D., Economic History of the Bombay Deccan and Karnatak (1818-1868), The Oriental Watchman, Poona, 1945.

2.   Choksey R. D., Economic Life in the Bombay Deccan, Asia Publishing House, Bombay, 1955

3.   Diddee Jayamala and Samita Gupta, Pune, Queen of Deccan, Elephant Design, Pune, 2002.

ACKNOWLEDGEMENT AND REFERENCES

4. Ghanekar P. K., Muthekathche Pune, Snehal Publication, Pune, 2015.

5. Gokhale Balkrishna Govind, Poona: In the Eighteenth Century an Urban History, Oxford University Press, Delhi, 1988.

6. Jadhav Rohan Vishwas, Role of Transportation in Urbanization of Poona (1804-1950), Notion Press, Chennai, 2023.

7. Khaire Nandita, etc. Ed., Merchants of Poona, Sakal Publications, Pune, 2014.

8. Mahajan Shantaram, Ed., Joshi Narayan Vishnu, Pune Shahrache Varnan, Mansanman Prakashan, Pune, 2002.

9. Maharashtratil Jilhe, Pune, Maharashtra State Government Publication Division, Mumbai.

10. Mangudkar M. P., Pune Nagarsanstha Satabdi Granth, Pune Mahanagarpalika, 1960.

11. Moledina M. H., History of Poona Cantonment 1818-1953, Poona and Kirkee Cantonments' Citizens' Association, Poona, 1953.

12. Newell H. A., Poona: The Peshwas city and its Neighborhood, Indian Army, Poona, 1918.

13. Oturkar R. V., Poona: Look and Outlook, The Poona Municipal Corporation, Poona, 1951.

14. Puranik Suprasad, Dnyat-Adnyat Pune, Merven Technologies, Pune, 2023.

15. Shakespear L. W., A Local History of Poona and its Battlefields, Macmillan and Co., London, 1916.

Webliography

1. https://map.sahapedia.org/inpune/1

2. https://pune.cantt.gov.in/history/

3. https://pune.gov.in/culture-heritage/

4. https://www.pmc.gov.in/en/heritage.

Introduction

Punyak, word comes from the word Punya i.e., merit / virtue. The region between the Sahyadri mountains shaped the geographical, political, economic, social, and cultural life of Pune. The city on the confluence of two rivers i.e., Mula and Mutha, played a crucial role in the settlement of humans in this area along with the rivulet like Nag and Ambil.

This timeline is titled timeline of Punyak, Poona, and Pune attempt to represent three significant era in the history of Pune. Punyak, literally translate into merit or virtue, symbolizes the early phase from 8th century common era onwards with minor variations. Poona, the colonial period name of the city, the period during which the city became cosmopolitan and people as well as goods from different corners of the world began appearing in the city. Pune, the name during the Peshwai and after the independence, used to identify the city. This is more than the name of the city also encompasses the culture and vibe of the city.

The Pune City served as a pivotal urban center for more than 1300 year all together, right from the Chalukyas, Rashtrakutas, Devgiri Yadavas, Bahamani, Nizamshahi, Adilshahi, Maratha State, Peshwai, British Colonial rule and even during Independent India.

This timeline tried to cover **very few, or some** events occurred in Pune city. Based on the sources mentioned in the reference list, this timeline is prepared for the readers. The dates mentioned in the booklet are as per Common Era (CE) time calculation.

The timeline of Pune is arranged in sequence of first year ranges followed by specific year, then some event's date are available in as happened month of that year, last the detailed date of the event occurred in specific year given in a format for example dd.mm.yyyy, as follows:

6th -10th century CE	Chalukya and Rashtrakuta dynasties ruled
1740s-60s	Karkolpura, from Karkol area of Karnatak, Brahmans use to come to Pune for receiving donation during Shravan Month and used to get settled temporarily at what we today call Sadashiv Peth
1793	Madhavrao II, donated land to Portuguese people for building Ornella Highschool and Church
December 1868	Construction of Khadakwasla Dam began
07.07.1910	establishment of Bharat Itihas Sanshodhan Mandal

The foundational work in the progress of the Pune city was made by the Bhosale family during the Shahjiraje Bhosale and his illustrious son Chhatrapti Shivaji Maharaj Shahjiraje Bhosale. The building of Lal Mahal and most importantly the assurance to the people for settling in the city and protection of their life and belongings.

Following is the flow chart depicting some key personalities from the Bhosale family:

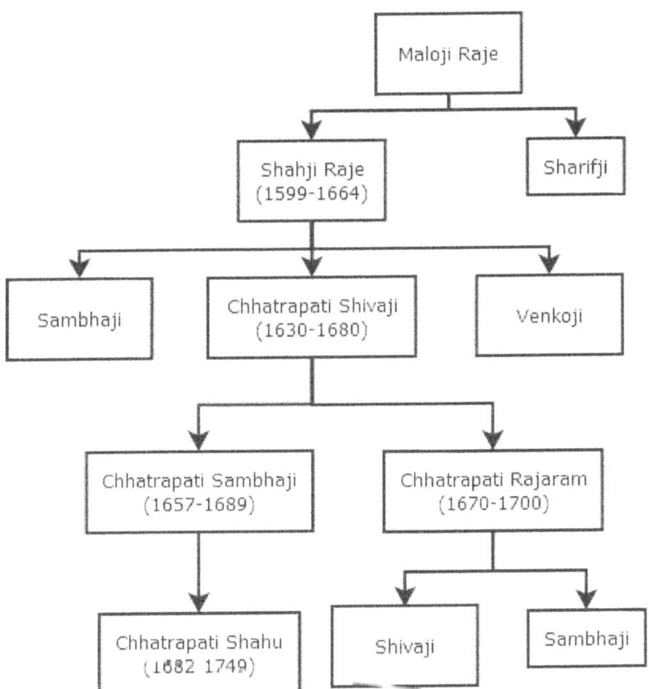

The developer of Pune city i.e. Peshwe family right from the Balaji Vishwanath Bhat, being Subedar of Pune and later the Peshwa of the Maratha State. Then Bajirao Balaji popularly known as Bajirao I or Thorle Bajirao Peshwe, made Pune as a permanent residence of the Peshwe family from 1730s onward and virtually political life of Indian sub-continent were operated from the Pune during heydays of the Peshwai.

Following is the flow chart depicting some key personalities from the Peshwe family:

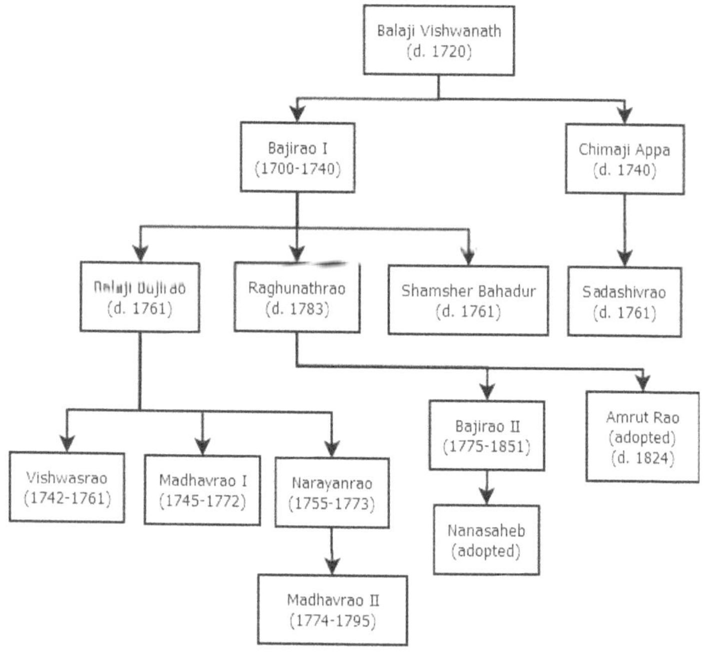

Date: 31ˢᵗ March 2025
Place: Pune

1. Timeline of Pune

758

Reference of Pune region as Punya Vishaya, cooper plate inscription of the Rashtrakuta King Krishna I.

760-973

The Rashtrakutas held the Pune Region.

768

Punaka reference in another inscription.

973-1184

Western Chalukyas held the Pune region.

1184-1300

Devgiri Yadavas holds the Pune region.

1290s

Narayaneshwar and Puneshwar were converted into Dargas now known as Thorla Shaikh Salla and Dhakla Shaikh Salla.

1300s

Poona region came under the control of Delhi Sultanate during Khalji and Tughlaq dynasties. Construction of Kille Hissar / Pandharicha Kot / Juna Kot by Bada Arab.

1510	Shri Chaitanya from Bengal, visited the city with his disciple Govinddas.
1590	*Punevadi* became Kasbe Pune.
1604	Sultan of Ahmednagar granted Pune to Maloji Bhosale, grandfather of Chhatrapati Shivaji Bhosale.
1625	Malik Ambar established Malkapur Peth.
1630	Deshpande of Pune, Moro Tandeo Honap revolted against Bijapur, to crush this rebellion Murar Jagdeo looted Pune.
1635	Shahjiraje Bhosale received Pune in Jahagir from Adilshahi.
1636-37	Shahjiraje Bhosale appointed Dadaji Kondadev as a in charge of Pune Jagir.
1636	Shahjiraje constructed Lal Mahal in Pune. Jija Bai Bhosale and Shivaji Maharaj moved in Lal Mahal.
1637-62	1. Kasba Peth. 2. Murtazabad-Shanivar Peth. 3. Malkapur-Ravivar Peth (redeveloped in 1740-41).

	4. Shahpura-Somvar Peth.
1659	Shahista Khan, Mughal Governor of Deccan occupied Pune.
1660s	Swargate was created to secure the entry point of city with Horsemen.
1663	5. Astapura-Mangalvar Peth.
05.04.1663	Night attack on Shahista Khan by Shivaji Maharaj.
1667	Pune restored to Maratha State.
1679	Administration of Pune were under Sachiv Naropant, from Chhatrapati Shivaji Maharaja's Council of Eight Ministers.
1685	Pune went into the control of Mughals.
1698	Balaji Vishwanath Bhat, Subhedar of Pune.
1703	6. Mohiyabad-Budhvar Peth Aurangzeb renamed Pune as Muhiyabad.
1707	Dhanaji Jadhav defeated Lodhi Khan, Mughal in charge of the city.
1708	Chhatrapati Shahu Maharaj received rights of collecting Chauth and Sardeshmukhi from Pune and administration remained in the hands of Mughals.

1717	Bahirat family sold half Patilki rights to Shirole family of Bhambhurda Village now known as Shivaji Nagar.
1720	Mughal rule was removed and only Maratha State continued. Bajirao I, became the Peshwa.
1721	Peshwas Bajirao I, appointed Bapuji Shripat as Subhedar of Pune.
31.03.1726	Pune given as a hereditary Inam to Bajirao I, by Chhatrapati Shahu.
1728	Bajirao I, ordered to pull down the walls of old fort in Pune. dismantling the old fort of Barya Arab and the land was handed over to Purandare and Chitnis.
1730s	Huzurpaga was set up for the cavalry of Peshwa. Malkapur Peth was renamed Ravivar Peth. Shahapur Peth renamed as Somwar Peth. Shastapur Peth was renamed as Mangalwar Peth. Muhiyabad Peth was renamed as Budhwar Peth by Bajirao I.
1730	Holkar Chhatri was built.

10.01.1730	Construction of Shaniwar wada began.
22.01.1732	Shanivar Wada Construction competed.
1734	7. Visapur-Shukravar Peth (redeveloped in 1748-49).
1736	Shaniwar Wada was constructed with 9 defence towers and 5 gates, only Northern entrance was uncompleted.
18.06.1738	Construction of Omkareshwar Mandir Completed.
1740s-60s	Karkolpura, from Karkol area of Karnatak, Brahmans use to come to Pune for receiving donation during Shravan Month and used to get settled temporarily at what we today call Sadashiv Peth.
1740	Balaji Bajirao became the Peshwa.
17.12.1740	Death of Chimaji Appa in Pune.
1747	Reference for 37 gardens in the city.
1748	Balaji Bajirao set up the Shukrawar Peth.
1749	Shri Siddheshwar Temple was built. Initiating the Construction of upper Katraj Lake.

April 1749	Balaji Bajirao constructed Devadeweshwar Temple on Parvati with Silver idol of Shiva and Gold idol of Parvati and Ganpati.
1750	8. Vetal-Guruvar Peth, Balaji Bajirao setup the Vetal Peth or Guruwar Peth. Permission for constructing Jain Tirthankar Parasnath temple was granted.
1752-55	Changed the course of Ambil rivulet, earlier it used to flow around, what we today call Bajirao Road. Initiate the setting up of Hirabag and Ranjan Mahal.
1753	Lake at Parvati
1753-55	Lake was constructed in the area that is today called as Sarasbag.
26.08.1754	Construction of Tri-shundya Ganpati Temple began.
1755	9. Nagesh-Nihal Peth. 10. Ganesh Peth (redeveloped in 1789). Construction of aqueduct from Katraj Lake to Pune. Water Lake was built at Parvati. Main Durbar Hall at Shaniwar

	Wada was Constructed called Ganapati Hall by Balaji Bajirao.
1755-57	Construction of Lower-level bigger Katraj Lake.
1756	Balaji Bajirao created Gosavipura in the Somwar Peth.
12.10.1756	Treaty of Poona, between East India Company and Peshwa, ceding 10 villages to company in Ratnagiri and not allowing Dutch in the Maratha territory, and opposing the Angrey, these were some terms of the treaty.
1758	Balaji Bajirao built the Ramana at Parvati.
1761	11. Narayan Peth. Madhavrao I, became the Peshwa Tulshi Bag was set up.
June 1761	construction of Lakadi Pul (Wooden Bridge).
23.06.1761	Death of Balaji Bajirao Peshwa at Parvati.
1763-65	Naro Appa setup the Tulshibag Shri Ram Temple.
May 1763	Nizam of Hyderabad sacked Pune.
1764	Construction of Nana Wada by Nana Fadnavis. Office of Kotwal was created; Balaji Narayan Ketkar became the first Kotwal of the city

1765	Vithal Mandir at Vithalwadi constructed by Sambhaji Gosavi. building of Bel Bag by Nana Phadnavis. Madhavrao I, ordered to conduct the survey for accounting damaged caused by the sack Nizam's Army. Govind Shivram Limaye (Khasgiwale) built the Rameshwar Temple. Total 923 Houses were reported
1766	Madhavrao, I established Nagesh or Nyahal Peth.
1767	12. Bhavani Peth.
1768	13. Muzaffarjang-Ghorpade Peth. British envoy got appointed at Poona.
12.04.1768	Madhavrao, I established Bhawani Peth for wholesale trade.
1769	14. Sadashiv Peth, Madhavrao I setup the Sadashiv Peth.
1770s	Haripant Phadke built Phadke Haud and Wada
1772	Narayanrao became the Peshwa.

1773	setup the Narayan Peth. Raghunathrao became the Peshwa.
30.08.1773	Murder of Naraynrao Peshwa at Shaniwarwada.
1774	Madhavrao II, became the Peshwa.
1779	Thana to Bor Pass Road fit for Artillery was constructed by British.
1780s-90s	Nana Phadnavis set up Garden in 18-acres land between Present day Natubag Area.
1780	estimated population of Pune was 01,50,000.
1781	15. Ghorpade Peth.
1782	Connected drainage system was set up to drain the water beyond the border of Pune at Kumbharwada called Gandhanala. Parvati Canals and Channels were constructed.
1783	16. Rasta Peth.
03.03.1783	Charles Malet, British Resident arrived at Pune.
1784	Madhavrao II, built the Ganpati Temple on the island in Lake, called as Talyatil Ganpati.

1786	Ghashiram Kotwal's son Jivanram received instructions from Peshwa to set up Navapura Peth (Navi Peth). Dullabhsheth Savkar built the Chaturshrungi Temple.
03.03.1786	Charles Warre Malet assumed his duties at Poona as British resident.
10.08.1786	Land for constructing Sangam Bungalow was assigned by Peshwa to British Resident.
1789	17. Nana. 18. Ganj (it is difficult to assign a date to this peth).
1791	Nana Phadnavis setup the Hanumant Peth for trading, later called as Nana Peth.
31.08.1791	Murder of Ghashiram Kotwal.
1792	Ganu Joshi build Nrusinha Mandir in his own bag (Garden).
1793	Madhavrao II, donated land to Portuguese people for building Ornella Highschool and Church.
1794	Mahadji Shinde Chhatri built by Mahadji Shinde.
1795	Pushkarni Water Tank was built near Vishrambag Wada.
04.12.1796	Bajirao II, became the Peshwa

22.02.1797	Malet resign from the post of British Resident of Poona.
1798	Sack of Pune by Bajirao II with the help of Shinde to raise money.
1799-1803	Construction of Shukrawarwada by Bajirao II.
25.10.1802	Battle of Poona Yashwantrao Holkar defeated the forces of Peshwa and Amrutrao became the Peshwa.
13.05.1803	Bajirao II, with the help of British was reinstalled as Peshwa of Pune.
1804	General Wellesley constructed a good military road from Bor pass to Pune.
1805	Area around Nrusinha Mandir received the status of Nrusinhapura Peth.
20.11.1808	Vishrambag Wada construction got completed.
1810	Wooden bridge on Mutha river damaged by flood and repaired cost Rs. 158, recovered from taxes. Pune had 412 temples. at the birth of Bajirao II's son, donations were made to approximately to more than 350 temples in the city and adjoining area.

1811	Asmani Mahal in Shaniwar Wada.
1813	Bajirao II constructed Budhwarwada, with Faraskhana, sub section for storing beds, carpets and allied objects.
1815	Murder of Gangadhar Shahstri, envoy of Baroda State.
1817	Khadki Cantonment established.
November 1817	Poona Cantonment established.
05.11.1817	Sangam Bungalow was destroyed by the forces of Peshwa. Battle at Khadki, British forces defeated Peshwa.
17.11.1817	Union Jack flag of British, hoisted on Shaniwarwada.
1818	Sholapur Bazur was established. Total 1048 houses were reported in the city. British built the City Jail at Khadak Mala, at the approximate place of Tofakhana of Peshwa and later the same place got converted into Mamlatdar office.
01.01.1818	Fall of Peshwa.
11.02.1818	Declaration by Elphinstone.
1819	£5000 i.e., Rs. 50,000 was the price of Dakshina for Educational purpose.

	Residence for Deccan Commissioner was built at Garpir Cantonment.
	Permanent Camp was enacted by Regulation I, 1819 at Poona Cantonment.
	William Chaplin was appointed as Commissioner.
	Elphinstone restored the lands and fortified Pandit Maharaj Gadhi to Bhaumaharaj Pandit.
1820s	estimated population of Poona was roughly around 01,00,000 to 01,13,000.
06.10.1821	A college for the encouragement of the study of Sanskrit and of ancient Hindu literature and science were opened with name Poona Sanskrit College was setup at old Vishrambaugh Palace.
1822	Khadki Bazar started.
1824	Sardar Sorabji Ratanji Patel Der-E-Meher was built.
1825	Vanavadi Bazar founded. St. Mary Church was built. Bishop Heber, First Bishop of Calcutta, visited Pune.
29.04.1825	First Parsi Tower of Silence was erected.

1826	Attempt was made to start on an experimental basis the production of silk by Captain Robertson, result in a discontinuation. First Marathi Primary school began.
1827	Boundaries for Poona Cantonment were mostly settled.
1828	first proper Government House was made by John Malcolm after purchasing house of Colonel ford (British trainer for Peshwa army) British ordered to demolish the Shukrawar Wada.
21.02.1828	Shaniwarwada burndown.
1830	Club of Western India got set up. 18 acres Garden of Nana Phadnavis was given to Balajipant Natu by British rule. Nivdungya Vithoba mandir was built.
17.06.1830	Inauguration of Wooden Wellesley Bridge or Sangam Bridge.
1831	Ghorpade Ghat was constructed.
1833	A. Dinshaw & Co., a clock and specs shop began in camp area, chronometers manufactured by company were also exported to England via ship.

1835	British repaired the water dam at Kumbhar Ves and widened the road on it. Ganesh Peth Bridge was constructed Over Nagzari Rivulet.
1836-40	Nagzari Bridge connecting Somwar and Mangalwar Peth
22.03.1838	Bijwar Vishnu Temple at Shaniwar Peth was constructed.
1840-45	Burdi Bridge connecting Bhawani and Raviwar Peth over Nagzari rivulet.
1840	Racecourse was built.
1842	Permanent barracks for European soldiers were built at Ghorpadi. English class attached to the Poona Sanskrit College Sir Jamsetjee Jejeebhoy Agiary was built.
31.01.1842	Administration of Parvati Temple went into the hands of Collector and committee of five members
1844	Ghorpadi Bazar founded.
1845	Ghaseti Bridge was constructed connecting Bhawani, Ganj and Vetal Peth. Bhati Gate Bridge was constructed in Rasta Peth.

07.02.1848   Pune Nagar Vachan Mandir
Library (old Name Poona Native
General Library) were set up.

1849   Infant school in Pune was set up
and students used to get Re. 1 as a
salary.

12.02.1849   Dnyanpraksh Newspaper began
its publication.

1850   Prohibited the organization of
Tamasha on roads.
Construction of Bund at
Yerwada.
Narpatgir Vishnu Mandir was
built.

1851   estimated population of Poona
was 73,209.
Closure of English newspaper
called Poona Chronical.
Establishment of Dakshina Prize
Committee.

17.09.1851   Second Girls School in Rasta
Peth was opened.

1852   First School for scheduled caste
people.

1854   College of Engineering Pune
started.
Telegraph line connected Pune
with Mumbai.
First attempt was made with the
initiative taken by District
Collector, for this Collector called

for an unofficial meeting of people living in Poona and explained them about 1850 Act and its usefulness to Poona. As outcome of the meeting, 1191 people with their signature sent a letter in May 1854 to Bombay government in Favor of forming municipality in Poona.

1855	Construction of St. Patrick Church.
12.01.1855	Post office in Pune got established.
15.03.1855	Third Girls School in Gurwar Peth was opened.
12.01.1856	Closure of Night Curfew Gun Fire.
1857	Sir Hugh Rose from Bombay army went to north India to aid the Bengal army in area, two Pontoon rafts, brought with great difficulty from Poona some eighteen hundred miles away, were floated by sunset on the Jumna and the Junction with the Bengal army effected at Calpee (Kalpi). Imposition of tax on influx of Horse, cattle and donkeys. 54 water tanks (Haud) were

	connected to Katraj water tap connections in the city.
20.05.1857	Bombay Government declare establishment of Poona Municipality.
01.06.1857	Poona Municipality start operating.
1858-80	Through 150 donkeys waste from city were collected and taken outside for disposing.
May 1858	Due to the 1857 revolt, actual functioning of Municipality began.
14.06.1858	Khandala-Pune Railway line opened.
1858	Establishment of Baptist Chapel.
1863	Residence for Deccan Commissioner at Garpir Cantonment destroyed by fire. Sir Bartle Frere put Leith as an in charge for preparing enquiry into the Sanitary conditions of Poona city Cantonment. The David Sasson Infirm Asylum was established.
1864	Estimated population was 80,000. The Bishop's high School was established.
1865	Total length of roads were 556 ½ out of it 142 were metaled and

334 were unmetalled.
Engineering College buildings were built.
St. Vincent Church was built.
Wittul Shamsett & Sons started a Jewelry and watch store in cantonment area, later after Independence entered in a business of crafting silvers trophies.
Orphan, differently abled, physically challenged and visually impaired home was created at Thosar Paga with the major contribution of David Sasson.
Layout of Botanical Garden was made.

1866	St. Paul Church was Build. Collection of Property tax began 4% of total rent of the property from a year after deducting 10% maintenance charges.
1867	Sassoon Hospital was constructed. The Cantonment Bazar now known as Shivaji Market was built. Fitzgerald bridge was constructed on Mula Mutha river at Bund.

29.09.1867	Ohel David Synagogue was constructed.
1868	Construction of Deccan College, with the donation from Jeejeeybhoy. Ganesh Vasudev Joshi built New Vishnu Temple in Sadashiv Peth.
December 1868	Construction of Khadakwasla Dam began.
1869-72	Mr. R. E. Light prepared survey map of Pune 200 feet to an inch.
1869	Khadki Ammunition factory was built. Bund Garden was set up. Municipality started collecting Octroi duty.
1870	Council Hall at Pune construction was completed. Prarthana Samaj founded. Daruwala Bridge was constructed over Nagzari rivulet connecting Somwar and Rasta Peth. Poona Training College for Women was started. Church of the Holy Name of Panch-Howd Mission was constructed.
02.04.1870	Poona Sarvajanik Sabha formed
1871	New Government House was completed at Ganeshkhind now

known as Main Building of Savitribai Phule Pune University. "Vicharavatee Stree Sabha" First Women's Association with 8 Members.
Vaktritvottejaka Sabha formed.
Yerawada Central Jail was constructed.

1872	Estimated population was 90,436. Zero Milestone was installed outside the GPO.
1873-74	General Post Office (GPO), building was completed.
1873	Mahatma Jyotiba Phule published Gulamgiri book, giving a historical survey of the slavery of lower castes.
25.04.1873	First public Haldi-Kunku Samarambha at Nava Vishnu Mandir built by Ganesh Vasudev Joshi.
24.09.1873	Satya Shodhak Samaj founded by Mahatma Jyotiba Phule.
1874	Maharashtra Education Society was established earlier known as Poona Native Institutions.
1875-76	Collection of Water tax began.
1875	Pune Industrial Museum constructed.

	Vasant Vyakhyan Mala was initiated by M. G. Ranade.
May 1875	Inauguration of Wellesley Bridge or Sangam Bridge built in stone.
1876-82	Mahatma Phule was a member of the Municipality.
1876	Famine hit the Pune area. Request for conducting Elections for Municipal body was made.
1876-78	Under the in charge of Major Francis detail survey map of Pune were prepared 50 feet to an inch.
07.07.1877	Construction of Pune Archive began.
1878	Dorabjee & Sons Restaurant in camp area, well known for serving authentic Parsi food. Municipality opened Its hospital with English medicine on the border of Narayan and Shaniwar Peth. Bairamji Jijeebhai (B. J.) Medical School (College) began.
1879	Vishrambagwada catches fire. Aryabhushan Bhavan was founded.
13.05.1879	Budhwarwada catches fire.
1880	The Gymkhana, now known as Poona Club, was built. Municipality opened hospital at

	Sadashiv and Nana Peth, Ayurvedic and English medicine respectively.
	Beginning of Deccan Education Society.
02.01.1880	Establishment of Poona New English School.
1881	Estimated population was 99,622.
02.01.1881	Beginning of English Newspaper called Maratha.
04.01.1881	Beginning of Marathi Newspaper called Kesari.
1882	Founding stone for the building of Theosophical Society at Pune.
	Municipality imposed tax on vehicles.
1883	Mahatma Jyotiba Phule published Shetkaryacha Asud i.e., the cultivator's whipcord, where he has analysed how peasants were being exploited in those days.
	Vithaldas Narayandas & Sons Sugandhi began their business in perfumes, fragrances, agarbatti and dhoop sticks.
	Women and differently abled people can assign their voting right to someone else called as Voting by Proxy.

	Shikshan Prasarak Mandil was formed.
01.01.1883	Establishment of Nutan Marathi Vidyalaya.
28.03.1883	First Election for Poona Municipality was conducted for 12 out 24 Members.
1884	Mahatma Phule Mandai (formerly Reay Market) opened.
	H.H.C.P. (His Highness Chintamanrao Patwardhan) female school also called as Huzurpaga girls School began.
	First President of Poona Municipality, from elected members was Sardar Dorabjee Padamji.
	20 out of 30 members were elected from people and 10 appointed by the Government in Poona Municipality, 4 seats were reserved for educated candidates and 16 were open for all.
12.02.1884	Poona Sub-urban Municipality formed with Government Notification.
1885	Fergusson College was established.
	Pune Industrial Museum renamed as Lord Ray Industrial Museum.
	Reay Market was Constructed.

Deccan paper Mill setup at Mundhwa.

Establishment of Poona Club.

Tulshibag Sansthan Shri Ram Mandir, some sections in the temple complex were converted into the Shops due to the financial constraints on the Sansthan for maintaining the premises.

1886   Prison Press at Yerwada.

Pune Nira section of railway line opened.

Mandai shifted to Reay Market now Mahatma Phule Mandai complex from open space in front of Shaniwar wada.

1888   Yerawada Village and Sangamwadi were incorporated in Poona Sub-Urban Municipality.

Construction of Aanandasharam by Mahadev Chimnaji Aapte.

The Poona Cotton and Silk manufacturing Company established later became Rajabahadur Motilal Poona Mill.

At the place of Budhwarwada, Budhwarbag was created.

Poona Metal works factory began for producing copper and Brass utensils by Anantrao Godambe.

1888	Sudharak was started by G. G. Agarkar.
	Photo Zinco Graphic Pres was started.
17.06.1889	Yerwada Industrial School was established.
09.12.1889	Government opened School for giving Trade, Industry and Business oriented education.
1890-1902	Waste collection and disposition were given on contract to private sector.
1890	The Camp Education Society was established.
04.10.1890	Ghorpuri to the Poona section of Madras and Southern Mahratta railway (Meter Gauge) Poona Branch of 00.91 miles opened.
1891	estimated population was 01,18,790.
	Ardeshir Sons, was founded manufacturing soda water and later introduced flavored soda water and built several Ice factories in Maharashtra.
	Abdul Wahed Urdu Primary School was founded.
1.09.1891	Construction of Pune Archives building was completed.
1892	Aga Khan Palace built by Sultan Mohammed Shah, Aga Khan III.

	Kaka Halwai began their business in Sweets, in 1918 Morappasheth Gadve started a sweet shop at present location near Datta Mandir.
12.02.1892	Establishment of Shree Varadmurti Devasthan or Gupchup Ganpati.
1893	Municipality opened Ayurvedic Hospital at Mahatma Phule Mandai. Raja Bahadur Spinning Mill became operational. Sardar Dastur Nosherwan Girls High School was started.
1894	Sugarcane research Centre at Manjari farm established. Bharat Natya Sanshodhan Mandir theatre company was started.
1895-97	Lokmanya Tilak was the member of the Municipality.
1895	Indian National Congress and Indian National Social Conference's annual session held in Poona. Lokmanya Tilak founded Shri Shivaji Fund Committee for celebration of Shiv Jayanti.
1896	At Hingne, Maharshi D.K. Karve Girls School and Widows' home were started.

	The dreaded bubonic plague made an appearance in Pune. Second idol of Shreemant Dagdusheth Halwai Ganpati temple began to celebrate and accepting public donations began.
04.11.1896	Formation of Deccan Sabha.
19.12.1896	First patient diagnosed with the Plague.
1897	Plague epidemic broke out in City.
10.02.1897	Officer Rand got appointed to restrict the outbreak of Plague.
22.06.1897	Murder of Officer Rand by Chaphekar Brothers.
1898-1906	Namdar G. K. Gokhale was a member of the Municipality.
1898	Kukreja and Co. Sports related equipment shop opened in camp area later the Madan brothers opened Sports equipment shop named Champion Sports. 20 out of 38 members elected from people and 18 members appointed by Government in Municipality.
1899	Navin Marathi Shala was established.
1901	Estimated population was 01,11,381.

	Shri. Kumthekar became the First Chief Officer of Municipality.
1902-05	Sir Visvesvaraya, Government appointed member of Municipality.
1902-27	Municipality experimented with waste disposition like charging money to contractors, producing fertilizers out of the waste, etc.
1902	Namdar G. K. Gokhale, became the President of the Municipality.
1904	Construction of Premal Vithoba temple by Bhimabai Devkar.
1905	Shankar Ramchandra company (SRC) was established as furniture manufacturing and renting company, some of the notable buyers are National Defence Academy, Council Hall and Savitribai Phue Pune University in Pune. Later, the company turned into an auctioneer firm during the time of Independence. Insect Museum was formed at the College of Agriculture.
12.06.1905	Servants of India Society was formed by G. K. Gokhale.
7.10.1905	Burning of foreign cloths by the initiative taken by Swatantraveer Vinayak Damodar Savarkar.

1906   Shri Mhalsakanta Mandir was built by Vishnu Bhave.
Maharashtra Sahitya Parishad was formed.
Deccan Gymkhana was founded.

1908   Paisa Fund Glass Works began at Pune because of the initiative taken by Antaji Kale to collect 1 paisa from the Indian to commence the Industrialization funded by common Indian masses.
Ranka Jewelers started their business in a rented space at Raviwar Peth by the name Gulabchand Chattaringji & Sons.
Darbar Brass Band began operational in Pune under the Shaikh Iqbal Shaikh Mohammed by the name The Universal Band Company.
Establishment of Ranade Institute.
Leprosy hospital was opened by Christian Missionary at Kondhwa.
The Depressed Classes Mission Society of India Poona Branch was formed by Vithal Ramji Shinde.

1.01.1908	College of Agriculture began in Pune.
1909	Somvanshi Mitra Newspaper began by Shivram Kamble.
	Tehmuljee Pundole started a humble watch repairing and selling shop in camp that later turned into CT Pundole & Sons international watch repairing and selling firm.
	Poona Anath Vidyarthi Gruha was established.
	The Deccan Agricultural Research Association was established.
02.10.1909	The Seva Sadan Society was established.
1910-19	Underground Drainage pipelines were installed.
1910	Construction of Central Building at Pune.
07.07.1910	establishment of Bharat Itihas Sanshodhan Mandal.
1911	estimated population was 01,17,256.
	Travelling cinema were introduced.
	Bharat Gayan Samaj was founded by Pandit Bakhale.
02.10.1911	Pune Marathi Granthalaya was established.

1912	26 out of 39 members were elected from people but 2 out of 26 were reserved for Income taxpayers. Sardar Dastur Nosherwan Boys High School started. The Poona Young Cricketers Hindu Gymkhana began.
1914	Establishment of Likte Rammandir. Khadki War Cemetery. Napier Cinema house was built now known as West End.
1915	Yerwada Central Mental Hospital started. Water Tanks at Swargate were constructed. Voting by Proxy was discontinued in Municipality elections. Pune started receiving Water from Khadakwasla Dam by taps. The Karnataka Sangh was started. The Church of Holy Angels was built.
October 1915	The ARS Inamdar Public Library is the central library of the Deccan Muslim Institute was established.
07.02.1915	Gangadhar Narhar Pathak built Aryan Cinema.

1916	New Poona College, now known as Sir Parshuram Bhau College, was built. Scheme for constructing Laxmi Road was sanctioned. Paterson rapid filter was installed to supply filtered water to Pune Cantonment. Shreemati Nathibai Damodar Thackersey Women's University began. Rajiwadekar Topiwale, began shop of Caps selling some handmade caps. Narayan Govind Rajiwadekar and his son, Manoharrao kept the blend of traditional and Modern caps in shop.
1917-50	Flushing toilets and drainage lines were installed in the city.
1917	Oppressed India Association founded by Shivram Kamble. Queen Mary's Technical School for Disabled Soldiers at Kirkee was established.
06.07.1917	Inauguration of Bhandarkar Oriental Research Institute.
1918	Turf Club house setup. Property tax was made 5% from earlier 4%, this was the only hike in the property tax during the

	1866 to 1947.
	The Deccan Institute of Commerce was established by Prof. G. K. Bhopatkar.
	The Shivaji Maratha Society was established.
	The Gopal Gayan Samaj Sangeet Mahavidyalaya was founded.
1919	Pune City Bharat Scout and Guide institute was formed in Nutan Marathi Vidyalay.
1920-53	Building of Laxmi Road.
1920s	Pensionwala Masjid was constructed.
1920-21	Electric Street lights were installed in the city.
1920	Death of Lokmanya Tilak. Jagganath Maharaj Pandit, donated the Maharaj Pandit Gadhi to create memorial for Lokmanya Tilak called as Tilak Smarak Mandir. Sathe Biscuit and Chocolate Co., Ltd. Began. Saraswati Mandir Sanstha was established. Muslim Students' Union was formed.

25.05.1920	Municipality passed a bill to move red light area outside the city, again in 1924 and 1954.
1921	Estimated population was 01,33,227. Shridhar Mahadev Gore started a Cloth shop named Gore & Mandali selling cotton, silk cloths, and cloths required for religious rituals. Reservation for educated and Income Taxpayers were discontinued, 43 out of 50 are now elected by people and 7 appointed by Government. Tilak Maharashtra Vidyapeeth was established.
19.11.1921	Inauguration of World War I memorial or Mahratta War Memorial in front of Shaniwar Wada later in 1931 moved to its present location at the end of Moledina Road.
1922	The Koregaon Park Estate incorporated in Poona Sub-Urban Municipality. Vidya Prasarini Sabha was started.
17.09.1923	Chhatrapati Shivaji Bridge (Formerly Lloyd Bridge) construction completed.

1924	Women can contest elections. The Deaf and Dumb Uplift Society was established by N. G. Gondhalekar. Indian Law Society's Law college was established. The formation of Maharashtreeya Mandal.
October 1924	The Poona Rigvedi Deshastha Shikshanottejak Sanstha was founded.
22.07.1924	Statue of Lokmanya B. G. Tilak was installed.
23.07.1924	Geeta Dharma Mandal was formed for teaching Karma yoga.
27.07.1924	Aadya Amruttulya was started.
1925-50	campaign for killing stray and rabid dogs, Municipality had given this task to Police department, giving poison to shooting them with bullet, these methods were executed.
1925	Sathe Biscuit and Chocolate Co. Ltd. Begin its operations with imported machines. Jaichand Karsandas Parekh started sweet shop called The fancy Indian Sweet Mart, later renamed to Bhavnagari Sweets. Sheth Tarachand Ramanath

	Ayurvedic Hospital was founded. The Poona Women's Council as branch of Bombay Presidency's Women council was formed. Brahman Karyalaya was established.
01.07.1925	Bombay-Poona railway line came directly under the control of Government from Great Indian Peninsular Railway Company.
1926	Shankar Balwant Kulkarni (Nanasaheb Kulkarni) started small shop of bicycles repair and oiling, later went on importing bicycles from England, USA, Germany and Japan. Acharya Kula was founded for training students in Vedantic Philosophy. Shri Vivekanand society was formed. The Poona Gujarati Kelvani Mandal was started.
1927-57	Waste dispositions were undertaken by Municipality by purchasing 120 Bullocks and 30 vehicles for transporting the waste.
1927	Saraswati Math was established to reduce illiteracy, improve sanitation and maternity center.

	The first Maharashtra Physical Education conference was held in the Pune.
05.01.1927	First All India Women's Conference met.
1928	Rajmachikar Flour Mill started its operation to grind different types of spices, etc., and is known for their authenticity.
02.02.1928	Municipality opposed the Simon Commission.
20.07.1928	Inauguration of Shimla office at Pune for monitoring Weather conditions called as Indian Meteorological Department, Pune.
30.10.1928	Pune District Court Building construction completed.
1929	The electrification of the Great Indian Peninsula Railway, main line, up to Poona from Kalyan, across the Ghats, was in Progress. Rigata Boating began. Adult Education League was established. Sadhu Vaswani Mission was started. National Institute of Naturopathy was founded.
October 1929	Parvati Satyagraha was organized by Dr. B. R. Ambedkar

1930	Servants of India Society became Gokhale Institutes of Economics. Municipality constructed Fish market and started giving licenses for selling fish and meat.
1931	Estimated population was 01,62,901.
01.01.1931	Vithalrao Dixit started Book shop called International Book service, at Deccan Gymkhana.
1932	Raghunath Desai started selling Mangoes grown on their farms in Konkan directly to customers in Pune by eliminating agents / middlemen. This turn into Desai Bandhu Ambewale known for their quality supply of Mangoes along with multiple byproducts of Mangoes. Shri Shivaji Preparatory Military School was established. Moldina Anglo-Urdu High School, began. Rashtriya Swayam Sevak Sangh began its activities in Pune. Gujar Cold drink began by Baburao Gujar.
February 1932	Modern Education Society was founded.
June 1932	Nowrosjee Wadia College was established.

01.01.1932	Beginning of Marathi Newspaper Sakal.
15.07.1932	Parvati and Ganpati's idol made up of Gold got stolen from *Parvati* Temple.
21.09.1932	Mohtarma Babajan Sultana Saheb passed away and later a dargah was constructed.
25.09.1932	The Poona Pact was signed between Mahatma Gandhi and Dr. B. R. Ambedkar.
1933	S. G. Gokhale & Co. was started by Sadashiv Gokhale to facilitate pandols for different social, political, religious, etc., gatherings.
	Prabhat Film Company shifted to Pune from Kolhapur, this film company was formed by Vishnupant Damle, Shaikh Fattelal, V. Shantaram, and Keshavrao Dhaibar.
17.02.1933	Pune Municipality requested the government to merge Poona and Sub-Urban Municipality, Khadki and Poona Cantonment to form one Municipal Corporation.
1934	Hight of Bund at Yerwada was reduced in April by 3 feet and again in May by 5 feet.
	New Education Society's Agarkar

	Girl's High School was started. Progressive Education Society was established.
February 1934	The Poona School and Industrial Home for the Blind was founded.
16.03.1934	The Mahratta Chamber of Commerce and Industries were formed.
1935	Laxminarayan Data came to Pune from Haryana started selling Chivda that later came to be known as Laxminarayan Chivda. Café Good Luck was started by Hussain Ali Yakshi at Deccan, earlier started tea stall at the same spot. The Hindu Women's Rescue Home Society was established. Ayurveda Rasashala was established. Bharat Natya Mandir theatre was constructed.
1936	Narhar Damodar, also called Nanasaheb Sarpotdar opened Poona Guest House well known for serving Maharashtrian food. George Restaurant was opened.
1938	Government appointed members were discontinued and all (60) members are now onwards elected by people.

	Bhandi Kamgar Sangh was registered for safeguarding interest of manufacturers.
01.06.1938	Continental Publisher was established by Gopal Patankar, Janardan Mahajan and Anant Kulkarni.
1939-40	Village Industries Experimental Workshop, on the ground of Agriculture college.
1939	Maratha History Museum at Deccan College shifted from Satara. Ahilyadevi High School for Girls was founded.
October 1939	Bangiya Sammeejan the Bengali Association was started.
17.05.1939	Tonga (Tanga) Owners association meet the Pune Municipality Chief for convincing, not to start the Motor bus service.
12.06.1939	Campaign for increasing adult literacy rate in city.
1940	Murudkar Zendewale began their shop in Pune of making different kinds of turbans. The Mahila Seva Gram was started. Gurudwara Shri Guru Singh Sabha was established.

	Deccan College's Archaeology Museum was established.
1941	Estimated population was 02,37,560., Silver Jubilee Motor Transport Company.
November 1941	The Andhra Association and Achanta Seshamamaba Telugu Library began.
01.03.1941	First public bus service began by the private company i.e., Silver Jubilee Motors Ltd.
1942	Scottish Missionary runed Kondhwa Leprosy hospital purchased by Government. Secret Radio Station was started for spreading Nationalism among people in Shukrawar Peth. The prevention of Food Adulteration Act of 1925 got implemented in the city. Bharatiya Sangeet Prasarak Mandal was formed and registered. establishment of Spicer Adventist University.
1943	Brihan Maharashtra College of Commerce was established.
24.01.1943	Bomb Explosion at Capitol Cinema Hall.
February 1944	Poona Philosophy Union was formed by Prof. Damle for

	reading and discussing philosophical studies.
01.04.1944	Railway lines in Poona city managed by Madras and Southern Mahartta Railway Company came directly under Government.
14.10.1944	Sangamwadi village transferred to Khadki Cantonment from Poona Sub-Urban Municipality.
1945	Sable Waghire & Company manufacturing beedi shifted to Pune and holds large share in total beedi production in India. Bazm-E-Khawateen, Poona Society of Ladies was founded.
1946	Maharashtra Association for the cultivation of science was formed. Poona Music Society was formed. Agharkar Research Institute was established.
1947	Establishment of Pune Leather works Co-operative Society Ltd. National Model School was founded. Shankar Maharaj Samadhi Math was built.
15.08.1947	India got the Independence from the British colonial rule.
1948	Vishnu Mani started his Manney's Booksellers shop in

	Camp area.
	Gulabrai Advani began Hindustan Book Stall in cantonment area.
	K-Pra Masale started by Kamalabai Bhat.
	Artificial limb Centre was started.
	College of Military Engineering was established.
May 1948	Armed forces Medical College was established.
01.06.1948	first nationalized State Transport Bus service inaugurated from Pune to Ahilyanagar then called as Ahmednagar.
1949	Maharashtriya Kalopasaka institution was established for the study of art and theatre.
16.01.1949	Establishment of Association for Abolition of Caste.
10.02.1949	Establishment of Savitribai Phule Pune University.
11.06.1949	Pune branch of Akhil Bhartiya Vidyarthi Parishad was established.
06.10.1949	Founding stone for the construction of National Defence Academy at Khadakwasala Pune by the hands of Prime Minister Jawaharlal Nehru.
1950	Approximate population of Poona city and suburbs reached

	4,00,000.
	Mirajkar Musicals, a shop for repairing and maintaining the musical instruments opened by Shamsuddin.
	Chitale Bandhu opened their sweet shop.
	Filtered water supply began to the city.
	Filtered water supply began to the city
	National Chemical Laboratory (NCL) was setup.
January 1950	establishment of Jayakar Library at Savitribai Phule Pune University.
15.02.1950	with the merger of Poona and Sub-urban Municipality, Poona Municipal Corporation was formed, all 21 age above people of Poona can vote.
01.03.1950	Poona Municipal corporation took over the Bus service from Silver Jubilee Motors Ltd.
01.04.1950	Garden Superintendent was appointed to look after all the gardens in the city.
1951	Hotel Roopali was started, earlier named as café Madras.
September 1951	Pre-Primary School was opened by the Government.

1952	First Master Plan for Greater Poona was proposed.
	Jangali Maharaj road was constructed.
	Kawre Cold Drink house was started.
	The National Institute of Virology was started.
	Defence institute of Advanced Technology was established.
4 and 6.03.1952	First election of Municipal Corporation with 65 Members.
26.03.1952	B. N. Sanas became the First Mayor of Pune and B. G. Parage Deputy Mayor.
02.04.1952	Shahu Swimming Pool was inaugurated.
1953-54	Municipal Corporation conducted medical checkup camps for students in Schools, Encouragement was given for initiating collection among students' like of coins, stamps, shells, envelopes, etc. Wanawdi Bridge was constructed connecting Wanawdi and Cantonment.
1953	Peshwe Park (Zoo) was setup by the Pune Municipal Corporation. Peshwe Park Bridge was Constructed.

	Aquarium at Chhatrapati Sambhaji Garden was built.
11.06.1953	Municipal Corporation runs high school became operational at Nana Wada.
09.11.1953	Mobile hospital service became operational in the city.
1955	Kayani Bakery was founded.
30.08.1955	Budhani Wafers shop was opened.
1956	Nana Wada High School ask their students to write their own Autobiography and submit to School.
	Dudhbhatti Bridge was constructed.
	Pangul ali Bridge was constructed.
	Kamala Nehru Park was established.
	Kwality Restaurant started.
	Central Gurudwara Sahib was built.
08.02.1956	64 out of 65 members resign for supporting Sanyukta Maharashtra.
08.04.1956	Children's Railway at Peshwe Park called Phulrani was inaugurated.

11.06.1956	Government run First Night School began functioning.
1957	Prabhat Chitranagari (Studio) sold to Indian Government. Government Polytechnic college was established. Vidyapeeth Buddha Vihar was established.
10.11.1957	Second elected Municipal Corporation came into existence.
1959	Indian Railway Institute of Civil Engineering (IRICEN) was established. The Pheonix Library was started. Tata Management Training Centre was started. The British Council Library was established.
12.07.1961	Panshet dam collapsed and flood occurred in Pune.
1962-65	Housing board constructed Lokmanya Nagar.
1962	Maharashtra Gandhi Smarak Nidhi Granthalaya was established. Raja Dinkar Kelkar Museum was established.
November 1962	The Indian Institute of Tropical Meteorology was established.
1964	Opening ceremony of Bal Gandharva Rang Mandir.

1965	Tribal Cultural Museum.
11.02.1965	Marz-O-Rin shop began
1966	Shreyas Dinning Hall started
1967	Poona Metropolitan Region was established.

2. Annexure A: Name Pune

Following is the list of name variations of Pune found in the various sources mentioning this area:

1. Punya Vishaya
2. Punaka Vishaya
3. Punaka Wadi
4. Punnaka
5. Purnaka
6. Punyapur
7. Purnanagar
8. Kasbe Pune
9. Punawadi
10. Puna
11. Punna
12. Poona
13. Ponah
14. Poonah
15. Pune

The name Punyak comes from the word Punya means merit or virtue. Geographically Pune is situated at the confluence of the Mula and Mutha rivers. These rivers originate in the Western ghats that meet each other in Pune and the area of their meeting is called Sangam i.e., Confluence. Alongside these rivers there were two temples called Puneshwar and Narayaneshwar, later during late 13th Century CE these temples were converted into Younger Sheikh Salla and Older Sheikh Salla.

The travelers or traders commencing their journey from the western coast traversing Sahyadri Mountain ranges with hard labor before railways and airways, coming to the region of Pune that facilitates water of Mula-Mutha confluence, plain fertile land and here onwards geographically speaking relatively convenient journey into the interiors of the Deccan. Due to these natural conditions the area might have been called as Punyak.

With time the minor variations in the name occurred and Kasbe Pune became the significant town with the amalgamation of three villages Kumbharli, Kasarli, and Punewadi. By the time of 1600s the Kasbe Pune turned into Kasba peth in the city called Pune and one after another 18 peths were added in the Pune during the 17th and 18th centuries. By different able administers of the Pune.

During the British colonial administration, Pune was called as Poona due to the convenience of pronunciation to the Britishers, and again after independence the Poona was renamed as Pune.

3. Annexure B: Population of Pune

The Pune city experienced diverse composition of population from the eighteenth century onwards as it was made residence of Peshwa from Bajirao I, onwards and the economic, political, and military nature for Pune of colonial State during British rule gave multi-cultural identity to the city.

Period from 1740 to 1780, the city experienced consistent rise in the population due to the political stability facilitated by the Peshwas. From 1780s onwards various internal and external factors i.e., nature of rule during Bajirao II, political and military factors involved due to the Peshwa, Holkar, Shinde and British relations with each other.

From the 1850s onwards the arrival of post, telegraph, railways and administrative reforms in terms of local government created suitable situations for the increase in the numbers of inhabitants of the city. Only in the last decade of the 19th century was there a little decrease in the population of Pune due to the spread of the Plague.

1950s, experienced growth in the total population of the city with merger of Poona Municipality and Poona Su-urban Municipality in the year 1950.

The following table depicts approximate numbers of population each year:

Sr. No.	Year	Population
1	1740	40,000
2	1780	1,50,000
3	1818	1,05,000
4	1822	78,000
5	1851	73,209
6	1864	80,000
7	1872	90,436
8	1881	99,622
9	1891	1,18,790
10	1901	1,11,341
11	1911	1,17,456
12	1921	1,33,227
13	1931	1,62,001
14	1941	2,37,546
15	1951	4,80,942
16	1961	7,22,518

4. Annexure C: Peths in Pune

The Peths in Pune city mark their distinct features with the legacy and characteristics they hold in their composition. The first i.e., Kasbe Pune later Kasba Peth established since 500s CE onwards. The Murtazabad, Malkapur, Shahpur, and Astapur setup during the Nizamshai and Adilshahi period, Mohiyabad set during the Mughal occupation of the city. Then onwards the Shukrawar, Gurwar, Nagesh, Ganesh, Ganj, Narayan, Bhawani, Ghorpade, Sadashiv, Rasta, Nana, and Navi Peth were established during the Peshwai period.

The following is the approximate timeline of the establishments of Peths in Pune[1]:

1625

Malik Ambar established Malkapur Peth

1637-62

1. Kasba Peth
2. Murtazabad-Shanivar Peth
3. Malkapur-Ravivar Peth

[1] *Gokhale Balkrishna Govind, Poona: In the Eighteenth Century, Oxford University Press, Delhi, 1988.*

	(redeveloped in 1740-41)
	4. Shahpura-Somvar Peth
1663	5. Astapura-Magalvar Peth
1703	6. Mohiyabad-Budhvar Peth
1734	7. Visapur-Shukravar Peth (redeveloped in 1748-49)
1750	8. Vetal-Guruvar Peth, Balaji Bajirao set up the Vetal Peth or Guruwar Peth
1755	9. Nagesh-Nihal Peth 10. Ganesh Peth (redeveloped in 1789)
1761	11. Narayan Peth
12.04.1768	Madhavrao, I established 12. Bhawani Peth for wholesale trade
1768	13. Muzaffarjang Peth
1769	14. Sadashiv Peth, Madhavrao I set up the Sadashiv Peth
1781	15. Ghorpade Peth
1783	16. Rasta Peth
1780s	17. Navi Peth
1789	18. Nana Peth

19. Ganj Peth (It is difficult to
assign date to this peth)

Following is the table depicting Year of establishment for
the Peth in Pune along with their old and new name:

Sr. No.	Year	Old Name	New Name
1	5th Century CE	Kasbe Pune	Kasba
2	16th Century CE	Murtazabad	Shanivar
3	1625	Malkapur	Ravivar
4	1637-62	Shahpura	Somvar
5	1637-62	Astapura	Mangalvar
6	1703	Mohiyabad	Budhvar
7	1734	Visapur	Shukravar
8	1750	Vetal	Guruvar
9	1755	Nagesh-Nihal	-
10	1755	Ganesh	-
11	1761	Narayan	-
12	1767	Bhawani	-
13	1768	Muzaffarjang	-
14	1769	Karkolpura	Sadashiv
15	1781	Ghorpade	-
16	1783	Rasta	-
17	1780s	Navapura	Navi
18	1789	Hanumant	Nana
19	-	Ganj	-

5. Annexure D: Gardens in Pune

The Pune during the 18th century under the Peshwai flourished as a major urban center in India and because of Political seat of the Maratha State, gardens were developed in and around Pune during the Peshwa rule. Approximately 37 gardens were reported in Pune during this period.

Following are some names of the gardens during Peshwa rule:

Hira, Saras, Vasant, Moti, Parvati, Bunglow, Wanwadi, Hingne, Ramana, Wadgaon, Manik, Pashan, Katraj, Kothrud, Bel, Tulshi, Nana later called Natu, etc.

During the colonial British rule Bund Garden, Empress, Budhwar, Sambhaji, Jijamata, Daruwala, Shivaji Park, Khadi Maidan, Powerhouse, Kumbharwada. These few gardens were set up during colonial rule. As a nature of colonial rule aesthetics for the benefit and health of the people of Pune city was not the priority of the government during British rule, the gardens of Peshwa period were neglected and firstly due to the removal of State patronage these gardens slowly and steadily disappeared and secondly the expanding city area required more space for constructing utility building like residential, commercial, administrative purposes. As a result of the combining effect of both causes the numbers and size of Gardens in Pune kept on shrinking during the colonial rule.

After Independence and the establishment of Pune Municipal Corporation till the concern time following gardens were set up in Pune:

Peshwe, Erandwana, Ghorpade, Shaniwarwada garden, Shivaji Talav (Swimming Pool) garden, Chhatrpati Shahu Garden. Around 18 Gardens were there at the time of 1950. The Pune Municipal Corporation created a post called Garden Superintendent on 1st April 1950 to look after all gardens in Pune.

6. Annexure E: Administrators of Pune

This Annexure attempts to give broad and approximate timeline of the administrators of Pune. Please note that only available names of Commissioners, Mayors, etc., are mentioned. This does not represent complete and continuous picture for the list of administrators of the Pune.

760-973	The Rashtrakutas held the Pune Region
973-1184	Western Chalukyas held the Pune region
1184-1300	Devgiri Yadavas holds the Pune region
1300s	Pune region came under the control of Delhi Sultanate during Khalji and Tughlaq dynasties
1400s	Bahamani Sultanante of Deccan controlled the region
1500s	Nizamshahi of Ahmednagar controlled the region

1604	Sultan of Ahmednagar granted Pune to Maloji Bhosale, grandfather of Chhatrapati Shivaji Bhosale
1630s	Adilshahi of Bijapur got the control
1635	Shahjiraje Bhosale received Pune in Jahagir from Adilshahi
1659	Shahista Khan, Mughal Governor of Deccan occupied Pune
1667	Pune restored to Maratha State
1679	Administration of Pune were under Sachiv Naropant, from Chhatrapati Shivaji Maharaja's Council of Eight Ministers
1685	Pune went into the control of Mughals
1703	Aurangzeb renamed Pune as Muhiyabad
1708	Chhatrapati Shahu Maharaj received rights of collecting Chauth and Sardeshmukhi from Pune and administration remained in the hands of Mughals

1720	Mughal rule was removed and only Maratha State continued. Bajirao I, became the Peshwa
1721	Peshwas Bajirao I, appointed Bapuji Shripat as Subhedar of Pune
31.03.1726	Pune given as a hereditary Inam to Bajirao I, by Chhatrapati Shahu
1740	Balaji Bajirao became the Peshwa
1761	Madhavrao I, became the Peshwa
1772	Narayanrao became the Peshwa
1773	Raghunathrao became the Peshwa
1774	Madhavrao II, became the Peshwa
04.12.1796	Bajirao II, became the Peshwa
1802	Amrutrao became the Peshwa
1803	Bajirao II, became the Peshwa

British Residents at Pune Court

1785-96	Charles Malet
1796-98	Joshua Uhthoff
1798-1801	William Palmer

| 1801-11 | Barry Close |
| 1811-19 | Mountstuart Elphinstone |

Commissioners and Collectors of Pune

1819	William Chaplin was appointed as Commissioner
1823	reference of Mr. Robertson as a collector of Pune District
1827	reference to the Sir L. Smith as collector of Poona
1867	reference of Dr. A. G. Frezer as a collector of Pune

President of Poona Municipality

1884	Sardar Dorabjee Padamji
1902	Namdar G. K. Gokhale
1917	Shri H. N. Apte

Mayors of Pune

1952	B. N. Sanas
1953	G. M. Nalawade
1954	S. D. Ursal

1955	B. N. Sanas
1957	B. L. Shirole
1958	R. V. Telang
1959	V. B. Gogte
1961	Rohidas Kirad
1967	N. G. Gore

● ● ● ●

About the Writer

Dr. Rohan Vishwas Jadhav, is a student of History, have completed his Bachlor of Arts (B.A.) with History Specialization, Master of Arts (M.A.) in History, Master of Philosophy (M. Phil.) and Doctor of Philosophy (Ph.D.) dissertation and thesis pertaining to the history of Pune during the British colonial period from the Savitribai Phule Pune University, Pune. Qualified for Maharashtra State - State Eligibility Test (MH-SET) and University Grants Commission's National Eligibility Test with Junior Research Fellowship (UGC NET-JRF).